CYCLOPS
SCOTT SUMMERS

EMMA FROST

TRIAGE
CHRISTOPHER MUSE

TEMPUS
EVA BELL

MAGNETO
ERIK LEHNSHERR

MAGIK
ILLYANA RASPUTIN

FABIO MEDIA

BENJAMIN DEEDS

UNCANNY X-MEN

VS. S.H.I.E.L.D.

BRIAN MICHAEL
BENDIS
WRITER

CHRIS
BACHALO
PENCILER, #19-22 & #25

KRIS
ANKA
ARTIST, #23-24

TIM
TOWNSEND

AL
VEY

JAIME
MENDOZA

MARK
IRWIN

VICTOR
OLAZABA

WAYNE
FAUCHER

JON
HOLDREDGE

MARC
DEERING

INKERS, #19-22 & #25

COVER ART: **CHRIS BACHALO & TIM TOWNSEND** (#19-20, #22-23 & #25), **ALEXANDER LOZANO** (#21) **AND KRIS ANKA** (#24)

CHRIS
BACHALO
COLORISTS, (#19-22 & #25) WITH
JOSE VILLARRUBIA (#19 & #22)

VC'S JOE
CARAMAGNA
LETTERER

XANDER
JAROWEY
ASSISTANT EDITOR

MIKE
MARTS
EDITOR

COLLECTION EDITOR: **JENNIFER GRÜNWALD**   ASSISTANT EDITOR: **SARAH BRUNSTAD**
ASSOCIATE MANAGING EDITOR: **ALEX STARBUCK** EDITOR, SPECIAL PROJECTS: **MARK D. BEAZLEY**
SENIOR EDITOR, SPECIAL PROJECTS: **JEFF YOUNGQUIST**
SVP PRINT, SALES & MARKETING: **DAVID GABRIEL** BOOK DESIGN: **JEFF POWELL & RODOLPHO MURAGUCHI**

EDITOR IN CHIEF: **AXEL ALONSO** CHIEF CREATIVE OFFICER: **JOE QUESADA**
PUBLISHER: **DAN BUCKLEY** EXECUTIVE PRODUCER: **ALAN FINE**

UNCANNY X-MEN VOL. 4: VS. S.H.I.E.L.D. Contains material originally published in magazine form as UNCANNY X-MEN #19-25. First printing 2015. ISBN# 978-0-7851-8938-1. Published by MARVEL WORLDWIDE, INC., a subsidiary of MARVEL ENTERTAINMENT, LLC. OFFICE OF PUBLICATION: 135 West 50th Street, New York, NY 10020. Copyright © 2015 MARVEL No similarity between any of the names, characters, persons, and/or institutions in this magazine with those of any living or dead person or institution is intended, and any such similarity which may exist is purely coincidental. **Printed in the U.S.A.** ALAN FINE, President, Marvel Entertainment; DAN BUCKLEY, President, TV, Publishing and Brand Management; JOE QUESADA, Chief Creative Officer; TOM BREVOORT, SVP of Publishing; DAVID BOGART, SVP of Operations & Procurement, Publishing; C.B. CEBULSKI, VP of International Development & Brand Management; DAVID GABRIEL, SVP Print, Sales & Marketing; JIM O'KEEFE, VP of Operations & Logistics; DAN CARR, Executive Director of Publishing Technology; SUSAN CRESPI, Editorial Operations Manager; ALEX MORALES, Publishing Operations Manager; STAN LEE, Chairman Emeritus. For information regarding advertising in Marvel Comics or on Marvel.com, please contact Jonathan Rheingold, VP of Custom Solutions & Ad Sales, at jrheingold@marvel.com. For Marvel subscription inquiries, please call 800-217-9158. **Manufactured between 3/27/2015 and 5/4/2015 by R.R. DONNELLEY,**

Born with genetic mutations that gave them abilities beyond those of normal humans, mutants are the next stage in evolution. As such, they are feared and hated by humanity. A group of mutants known as the X-Men fight for peaceful coexistence between mutants and humankind. But not all mutants see peaceful coexistence as a reality.

UNCANNY X-MEN

Cyclops is the public face of what he calls the new mutant revolution. Rededicating himself to the cause of protecting the mutant race, he has begun to gather and train a new generation of young mutants.

Recently, a new brand of Sentinels has been attacking the Uncanny X-Men at every turn. Cyclops has reason to believe S.H.I.E.L.D. is behind these attacks, and he has become increasingly wary of venturing outside the safe confines of the New Xavier School. While on a recent training mission, the new mutant Hijack unwittingly alerted S.H.I.E.L.D. to the students' location. Although they were able to escape, Hijack was expelled from the school for his reckless actions. But the question remains: Where are these new Sentinels coming from?

ATLANTA.

GOOD MORNING, DAVID.

GEEZ!

DON'T BOTHER TRYING TO USE YOUR HIJACKING POWERS BECAUSE WE'VE HAD THE ENTIRE NEIGHBORHOOD'S VEHICLES TOWED AWAY.

EVERYTHING.

CARS, TRUCKS, BOATS, BICYCLES, TRICYCLES...

...THERE IS NOTHING FOR YOU TO USE, HIJACK.

AND, EITHER WAY, THERE'S NO REASON FOR YOU TO TRY TO ATTACK ME OR MY MEN.

WE'RE NOT HERE TO HURT YOU...WE'RE HERE TO HELP YOU.

MY NAME IS MARIA HILL.

SO, TELL ME--WHERE IS SCOTT SUMMERS?

TA-DAA.

ALISON BLAIRE, DAZZLER, AGENT OF S.H.I.E.L.D.

TRAITOR TO HER PEOPLE.

WHY DON'T YOU GUT HER?

I'M NOT DONE WITH HER YET.

EVERYONE HAS A PURPOSE.

I'M-- I'M NOT A TERRORIST.

I KNOW THAT.

I DIDN'T SAY YOU WERE, BUT...OH, THAT'S RIGHT.

DIDN'T YOU USE YOUR MUTANT POWERS TO TAKE A S.H.I.E.L.D. HELICARRIER FOR A JOYRIDE?

THAT SOUNDS A *LITTLE* TERRORIST-ISH TO ME.

I *DO* NEED A LAWYER.

ALL YOU NEED IS TO TELL ME EVERYTHING YOU KNOW ABOUT SCOTT SUMMERS AND THE X-MEN AND THIS MUTANT REVOLUTION HE HAS PLANNED.

BECAUSE, MR. BOND, I HAVE THE LEGAL RIGHT TO DETAIN YOU...

...FOR, LIKE, *EVER.*

I HAVE HER EYES AND EARHOLES PRETTY CLOGGED UP AND SHE IS MEDICATED ALL THE WAY UP TO HER DYE JOB...

...BUT *DAZZLER* HERE TURNS SOUND INTO LIGHT AND I DON'T REALLY KNOW HER LEVELS OR WHAT TRIGGERS HER POWERS.

SO LET'S KEEP IT TO A WHISPERY WHISPER.

WHAT YA DOIN'?

IT'S HER FAULT, REALLY...

...SHE'S THE ONE THAT SIDED WITH THE HUMANS AGAINST US.

"S.H.I.E.L.D. MUTANT LIAISON."

THAT'S THE MOST *DISGUSTING* THING I'VE EVER HEARD.

THE HELL IS *THAT?*

I'VE BEEN LIVING AS HER AND I CAN TELL YOU FROM A FIRST PERSON POINT OF VIEW EXPERIENCE THAT SHE IS A SELLOUT DIRTY WHORE.

AND YOU AND I, VICTOR, WE HAVE KNOWN SOME DIRTY WHORE SELLOUTS IN OUR TIME.

YA DIDN'T ANSWER MY QUESTION, RAVEN.

YOU REALLY DON'T KNOW WHERE MUTANT GROWTH HORMONE COMES FROM?

THIS IS WHERE YOU'RE GETTING IT FROM?

OW.

DAVID, SCOTT SUMMERS *ABANDONED* YOU.

BUT I'M NOT STUPID. I KNOW HOW SMART HE IS.

RAISED AND TRAINED BY CHARLES XAVIER *AND* MAGNETO.

HE IS A RUTHLESS SON OF A BITCH.

HE DAMN WELL KNEW WE WOULD COME HERE FOR YOU.

HE *KNEW* WE WOULD BE WATCHING YOUR APARTMENT...

...*AND* EVA BELL'S PARENTS' HOME...

...*AND* FABIO MEDINA'S...

...AND CHRISTOPHER MUSE'S AND BENJAMIN DEED'S OLD DORM ROOM.

HE KNEW HE WAS *LITERALLY* DROPPING YOU OFF INTO OUR HANDS.

HE DID THIS TO YOU ON *PURPOSE.*

HE *MADE* THIS CONVERSATION HAPPEN.

I HAVE TO HAVE IT WITH YOU. I *HAVE* TO.

HE IS WORKING US LIKE PUPPETS, BUT I *HAVE* TO ASK YOU...

...AND IF YOU DON'T ANSWER I *HAVE* TO PUNISH YOU.

HE DID THIS TO US.

WHERE IS SCOTT SUMMERS?

OH.

WHAT IS IT?

IT'S A NEW MUTANT.

WOW. A VERY BIG ONE.

BIG?

POWERFUL.

WE SHOULD GO.

WHAT WERE YOU GOING TO SAY?

WE-- WE SHOULD GO.

YOU CAN TELL ME.

IF YOU HADN'T COME RESCUE ME WHEN YOU DID...

...WHO KNOWS WHAT SHAPE I WOULD BE IN.

LET'S FIND AND HELP OUR NEW MUTANT.

TO ME, MY X-MEN!

WHOA!

WHAT IS *THIS* NEW TRICK, ILLYANA?

I THINK THESE NEW SENTINELS ARE DOING SOMETHING TO OUR MUTANT POWERS.

THIS ISN'T MY MUTANT POWERS. THIS IS MY SORCERER'S POWERS.

SINCE WHEN DID YOU GET THIS GOOD?

I'VE BEEN WORKING WITH DOCTOR STRANGE IN MY SPARE TIME.

OH.

OKAY.

WELL DONE.

WHEN WERE YOU GOING TO TELL ME ABOUT THIS?

HE MEANS, "THANK YOU."

HOW ARE WE STILL ALIVE FROM THE *FIRST* ATTACK?

EVA THREW UP A TIME BUBBLE.

SHE GOT US OUT OF THERE.

JUST ABOUT A MINUTE'S WORTH.

TIME BUBBLE? DID--DID WE JUST *TIME TRAVEL?*

WELL DONE.

YOU HAVE TO TELL HIM.

...AVE WE LEARNED ...OTHING FROM RECENT EVENTS?!

MUTANTS SHOULD NOT *TIME TRAVEL!*

(EVEN A MINUTE'S WORTH.)

WHATEVER THAT MEANS!

REALLY.

OH HEY! MY BALLS ARE WORKING AGAIN.

WORDING!

MY MUTANT POWERS ARE UP, TOO.

GET THE STUDENTS OUT OF HERE WHILE I RIP THAT GIANT THING DOWN TO THE--

UNCANNY X-MEN #20 VARIANT
BY ADI GRANOV

WHERE IS *SCOTT SUMMERS*, MR. BOND?

I. DON'T. KNOW.

WHERE IS SCOTT SUMMERS?

STILL DON'T KNOW.

WHERE IS SCOTT SUMMERS?

I DON'T KNOW!

I DON'T BELIEVE YOU.

CLEARLY.

HERE'S THE THING, MR. BOND--ONE WAY OR ANOTHER SCOTT SUMMERS IS GOING TO REVEAL--

UM, DIRECTOR HILL?

WE FOUND HIM.

SCOTT SUMMERS AND HIS X-MEN ARE IN *CHICAGO*.

WE HAVE POSITIVE *SAT COMMAND ID*.

AND THERE WAS *ANOTHER* SENTINEL STRIKE ON THEM, AS WELL.

RIGHT NOW?!

YES, MA'AM.

AGENTS ARE HEADED TO THE SCENE. AS IS LOCAL LAW ENFORCEMENT.

S.H.I.E.L.D. HELICARRIER.
FLOATING WORLD HEADQUARTERS OF
THE U.N. PEACEKEEPING TASK FORCE.

1000 FEET OVER
AKRON, OHIO.

I DON'T *CARE* ABOUT WHO HAS WHAT POWERS! I CARE ABOUT US BEING *SMARTER* THAN HIM.

AND TO BE SMARTER THAN HIM WE HAVE TO THINK *TEN STEPS* AHEAD OF HIM!

HOW IS THAT WORKING OUT FOR YOU?

SCOTT SUMMERS, YOU'RE UNDER ARREST.

SURE I AM.

HEY, MY PEOPLE WERE ATTACKED BY MUTANT HUNTING SENTINELS.

AGAIN.

MUTANT HUNTING TECHNOLOGY THAT S.H.I.E.L.D. BOUGHT AND PAID FOR.

S.H.I.E.L.D. HAD *NOTHING* TO DO WITH IT.

I'VE BEEN INVOLVED WITH PSYCHICS FOR A VERY LONG TIME.

YEAH? NO KIDDING.

I KNOW THAT THE STORY THE GIRLS JUST PULLED OUT OF YOUR HEAD COULD HAVE BEEN IMPLANTED THERE SPECIFICALLY FOR THEM AND ME.

TO DISTRACT ME.

UNTIL SUCH TIME AS YOU CAN PROVE TO ME YOU ARE NOT EVEN PARTIALLY TO BLAME FOR ALL OF THIS MADNESS AGAINST MY PEOPLE, CONSIDER US AT WAR.

YOU'RE TRESPASSING ON MY SHIP.

NO, I'M NOT.

I'VE—I'VE JUST BEEN COMPROMISED.

MA'AM?

I WAS JUST PSYCHICALLY ASSAULTED.

GO TO CODE RED. WE'RE UNDER ATTACK.

I SAID GO TO CODE RED.

WE'RE UNDER--

YOUR MOVE, MS. HILL.

MADRIPOOR.

FREDERICK, WHAT ARE YOU DOING?

YOU LOOKIN' FOR A *SMACK*?

DID YOU NOT THINK WE'D NOTICE THE BROKEN LOCK?

OR THAT I COULD SMELL YOU A *BLOCK AWAY* EVEN IF I DIDN'T HAVE M MUTANT SENSES?

I-I JUST NEEDED MORE.

I FEEL IT SLIPPING AWAY AGAIN.

I NEED MORE.

I TOLD YOU, IF YOU NEED MORE *MGH* YOU COME TO ME.

YOU GONNA KILL ME NOW?

ALL YOU HAVE TO DO IS ASK.

WE'RE A TEAM. WE'RE A FAMILY.

I WANT YOU TO BE AS POWERFUL AS YOU CAN BE.

GOD CREATED YOU AS THE BLOB. YOU DESERVE YOUR POWER.

IT'S NOT YOUR FAULT THAT THE CRAZY WORLD TOOK THOSE POWERS AWAY FROM YOU.

BUT YOU NEED TO TRUST ME.

I-I DO.

THIS IS NOT TRUST, FREDERICK.

I-I-I-I JUST DIDN'T KNOW WHERE YOU WERE GETTING IT FROM.

I DIDN'T KNOW IF--

AND NOW THAT YOU DO, DOES IT MATTER?

DAZZLER BETRAYED OUR PEOPLE.

INSTEAD OF LETTING VICTOR HERE GUT HER FOR HER SINS...SHE'S SUPPLYING US WITH EVERYTHING WE NEED TO MAKE THIS ISLAND A TRUE MUTANT UTOPIA.

AND TO KEEP YOU THE WAY YOU HAVE BEEN AND SHOULD BE ACCUSTOMED TO BEING.

I'M SORRY.

HE'S ON THE MOVE.

HELICARRIER, DO YOU READ?

I REPEAT, DAVID BOND, A.K.A. *HIJACK*, IS ON THE MOVE.

WE LEARNED SOMETHING *IMPORTANT* TODAY.

OUR ENEMY UNDERSTANDS CEREBRO MUTANT TRACKING TECHNOLOGY.

THEY USED IT TO *LURE* US OUT.

THAT IS HOW THE ATTACKS ARE ALWAYS SO CLOSE TO US DISCOVERING A NEW MUTANT OR MAKING A PUBLIC APPEARANCE.

I THOUGHT IT MIGHT BE A PSYCHIC ATTACK, BUT NO...THEY ARE TRACKING US THROUGH *THIS*.

I THINK YOU'RE RIGHT.

CAN I GET THAT IN WRITING, MISS FROST? IT'S THE FIRST TIME YOU'VE SAID IT IN *YEARS*.

AND YOU RUINED THE MOMENT. AGAIN.

WOULD YOU LIKE *THAT* IN WRITING?

SO WHO ALL KNOWS HOW THIS CEREBRO THING WORKS?

MAGNETO.

CHARLES XAVIER.

THEY INVENTED IT.

PROBABLY TONY STARK.

HANK MCCOY.

REED RICHARDS.

TO HAVE A *TALK* WITH MY OLD BLUE FURRY BUDDY.

I'D LIKE TO COME AS--

--WELL.

AND HE'S GONE.

CUT OFF FROM OUR PEOPLE, OUR LEADER HAS LEFT US...

THAT DOESN'T FEEL *TOO* SYMBOLIC.

SO YOU ALL UNDERSTAND... MR. SUMMERS CALLED FOR A REVOLUTION.

BUT THIS IS NOW A *WAR*.

BE READY FOR ANYTHING. AT *ANY* TIME.

COMMANDER HILL, WE FOUND *SCOTT SUMMERS* ON SATELLITE!

WE HAVE HIM!

ALL STATIONS! FULL BATTLE ALERT.

I WANT SCOTT SUMMERS UNDER ARREST AND IN PRISON *TONIGHT!*

UNCANNY X-MEN #21 VARIANT

BY TERRY DODSON & RACHEL DODSON

21

THE
ORIGINAL!

AND YOU
WILL RESPECT
ME--*NN!*

HUAAGH!

OH NO.
NO NO
NO...

BEEP
BOOP
BOOP

COME ON, COME
ON, MYSTIQUE--
ANSWER!

YOU
PROMISED
ME.

YOU
PROMISED
YOU'D TAKE
CARE OF
ME!

YOU
PROMISED...

DAZZLER? CAN YOU HEAR ME?

... MAGNETO?

NNNNDON'T...

I WILL HELP YOU PAY THEM BACK FOR WHAT THEY'VE DONE TO YOU.

HOW LONG-- HOW LONG HAVE I-- WHOA...

SLOW DOWN.

WHO? WHO DID THIS TO ME?

IT'S NOT YOUR DECISION, HENRY.

IT IS A MUTANT PROBLEM AND THE MUTANTS WILL TAKE CARE OF IT.

SCOTT SUMMERS IS THE WORLD'S PROBLEM...

...AND S.H.I.E.L.D. IS THE WORLD PEACEKEEPING TASK FORCE.

RESPECT OUR AUTHORITY, DOCTOR.

STAND DOWN.

OKAY, YOU HAVE AN HOUR.

MISS HILL, YOU MADE ME SPECIAL MUTANT LIAISON. YOU REALLY SHOULD LET *ME* HANDLE THIS.

I'M GIVING YOUR PEOPLE A FAIR CHANCE, AGENT BLAIRE.

ISN'T THAT WHAT YOU WOULD WANT?

MISS HILL, ALL DUE RESPECT, SOMETHING IS THE MATTER WITH THEM.

SOMETHING OR SOMEONE HAS TAMPERED WITH THEM, AND I HAVE THE EQUIPMENT AND WHEREWITHAL TO FIGURE OUT WHO AND HOW IN MY LAB.

WE HAVE LABS AND SCIENTISTS, TOO.

PLEASE. SOMETHING IS *WRONG* HERE.

THIS IS ABOUT MUTATIONS. THIS IS WHAT I DO!

SCOTT SUMMERS NEEDS TO BE LOCKED AWAY.

UH-HUH.

DOCTOR, YOU HAVE ONE HOUR.

BUT SEE THOSE?

THEY ARE POINTING AT YOU.

THEY ALWAYS ARE.

I KNOW I'M PROBABLY BEING GREEDY, BUT ALL THE MAJOR PLAYERS IN ONE PLACE AT ONE TIME. HOW CAN I PASS IT UP?

TAK TAK TAK TAK

WE KNEW THIS DAY WOULD COME, DR. McCOY.

TAK TAK TAK TAK TAK

TAK TAK TAK TAK

TAK

STOP READING MY MIND, CELESTE.

WE'VE BEEN LOOKING ALL OVER FOR YOU.

JUST *ASK* ME WHAT I'M THINKING.

WELL, ONE HARDLY HAS TO READ YOUR MIND TO KNOW YOU'RE UPSET THAT PROFESSOR CYCLOPS LEFT WITHOUT YOU AND THAT YOU FIND YOURSELF UNCHARACTERISTICALLY WORRIED FOR HIM.

YOU'RE BOTH WORRIED FOR HIM AND ANNOYED BY HIM.

MINDEE...

AND YOU'RE FRUSTRATED BY THE CONTRADICTING EMOTIONS.

PLUS YOU CAN'T TURN ON CEREBRO TO TRACK HIM.

SOMETHING'S WRONG. I CAN FEEL IT.

WE COULD TURN ON CEREBRO FOR JUST, LIKE, SECOND AND SEE WHAT WE CAN FIND OUT.

WHAT IS THAT?

UNCANNY X-MEN #19 ANIMAL VARIANT
BY GIUSEPPE CAMUNCOLI & MARTE GRACIA

22

STEPFORDS, GIVE ME SOME PSYCHIC INTEL.

THERE'S SOMEONE IN THERE, MISS FROST-- BUT THEY'RE BLOCKING OUR PSYCHIC PROBE.

THERE'S SOMEONE *ELSE* IN THERE, TOO. HURT. UNCONSCIOUS.

THEIR THOUGHTS-- THEY'RE SCRAMBLED LIKE THEY'RE IN SOME KIND OF HAZE.

DIAMOND UP, STEPFORDS. EVERYONE ELSE BRACE FOR ATTACK.

FOLLOW ORDERS.

UM, MISS FROST?

ON MY ORDER, AND NOT BEFORE.

MAGNETO?!

SHE NEEDS HELP! BOY! HEALER! TO ME, NOW!

WHAT HAPPENED TO HER?

MYSTIQUE HAPPENED TO HER.

DEAR GOD...

IT'S WORSE THAN YOU THINK, EMMA. THE MUTANT HAS FALLEN PREY TO HER DARKER INSTINCTS...

...MAYBE WORSE THAN YOU OR I IN OUR MORE NOTORIOUS DAYS.

WHO IS THIS?

NO TALK. HEAL.

I'M HEALING. I'M HEALING.

WHAT'S HAPPENING?

SOMETHING'S WRONG...

MAYBE WE NEED TO GET HER TO A HOSPITAL.

SHHH...

AAGH!

ARE YOU OKAY, DAZZLER?

OKAY? AM I OKAY?

MYSTIQUE KIDNAPPED ME AND REPLACED ME IN MY WORLD.

AND SHE USED MY MUTANT DNA TO SYNTHESIZE MGH TO FUND HER MADRIPOOR OPERATIONS.

AND SHE'S STILL OUT THERE.

AM I OKAY?!

YOU SAVED MY LIFE, ERIC.

CATCH YOUR BREATH.

YOU'VE BEEN THROUGH A LOT.

EASY.

GET ME A WALKMAN!

A WHAT?

MUSIC! I NEED MUSIC.

WHAT KIND OF MUSIC?

REALLY. LOUD. MUSIC.

SCRRCHH

WHAT IS THAT?

I THINK THIS IS IT.

IT LOOKS LIKE S.H.I.E.L.D. IS FINALLY HERE FOR THE X-MEN.

DAY-UM. WELL, WE KNEW THIS DAY WOULD COME.

YEAH, UH, I THINK WE SHOULD ALL GET INSIDE.

Y'KNOW, I THINK YOU'RE--

UH... WHERE'S MY CAR?

IT'S ADVANCED TECH. YEARS AHEAD OF WHERE THEY ARE NOW... BUT DEFINITELY WHERE IT IS ALL GOING.

I SHUT THEM DOWN IN YOUR SYSTEM. YOU CAN LOOK FORWARD TO SOME NASTY DIARRHEA.

BUT IT HAD A VERY POTENT SIGNATURE.

I CAN, AND HAVE, TRACED IT BACK TO ITS OWNER. AND I KNOW WHO IT IS AND WHERE THEY ARE.

SHOW ME!

MAGIK, NO--WE NEED BACKUP!

BUT--

GET EVERYONE AND GET BACK HERE!

WHO?! WHO IS IT?

NEW SECRET XAVIER SCHOOL.

WHERE ARE WE GOING, MISS FROST?

WE ARE GOING TO FIND AND HELP SCOTT SUMMERS AND ILLYANA.

I SHALL JOIN YOU.

YEAH, YOU SHALL, MAGNETO.

WE NEED BOTH OF YOU. DAZZLER, ARE YOU UP FOR THIS?

THAT'S ALL I AM!

AND NOW MAGIK, APPEARING OUT OF NOWHERE.

OH GOOD, MAGNETO, DAZZLER...WE NEED ALL THE HELP WE CAN GET.

WHAT IS IT?

S.H.I.E.L.D. VERSUS THE X-MEN. COME WITH ME.

EVERYONE READY?

YES! GO! NOW!

I'M SORRY, HANK.

I'M TORN, FRANKLY.

AMAZING. HE JUST HUDDLED HIMSELF IN THE BOWELS OF AN ABANDONED HELICARRIER AND--

WAIT...

00:18

00:17

MAGIK! HIJACK! MY LOCATION!

WHAT?

THAT!

THE COUNTING DOWN THING?!

YES!

00:07

OH #$%&!

UNCANNY X-MEN #23 GUARDIANS OF THE GALAXY VARIANT
BY ARTHUR ADAMS & JASON KEITH

23

THE LAST WILL
AND TESTAMENT OF
CHARLES
XAVIER.©

CITIZENS, THIS IS S.H.I.E.L.D. COMMAND!

WE ARE UNDER SKRULL ATTACK.

PLEASE STAY IN YOUR HOMES!

DO NOT TRUST ANYONE!

MADRIPOOR.

"DAZZLER, MYSTIQUE IS NOT HERE."

IF SHE IS HALF AS SMART AS WE KNOW SHE IS... SHE IS *ANYWHERE* BUT ON THIS ISLAND.

MAGNETO...

THIS *IS* HER VERSION OF A MUTANT PARADISE. BUT SHE KNOWS TH WE, AND S.H.I.E.L.D ARE LOOKING FOR HER NOW.

ALISON, BE ANGRY. YOU *SHOULD* BE ANGRY.

SHE KIDNAPPED YOU, SHE IMPERSONATED YOU, MADE *MUTANT GROWTH HORMONE* FROM YOU.

WE'RE HERE BECAUSE WE WANT TO WATCH YOU BEAT THE BLUE OFF OF HER.

SCOTT...

...LOOK AROUND YOU.

I'M BEGGING YOU, SON, STOP THIS NOW.

THAT IS ENOUGH!

YOU ARE *NOT MY* FATHER.

PROFESSOR?

ARE YOU ALL RIGHT?

I'M FINE, MS. BELL.

YOU SURE?

OUR LAST "ADVENTURE" HAD ME INFECTED WITH *NANOTECH SENTINELS.*

THEY HAVE BEEN PURGED FROM MY SYSTEM, BUT IT ALL LEFT ME FEELING A LITTLE...FLUISH.

NANOTECH? SO LIKE REALLY SMALL?

YES.

CRAZY.

YES.

CAN I GET YOU SOMETHING?

HAVE YOU MUSTERED UP THE COURAGE TO TELL ME WHAT HAS HAPPENED TO YOU?

UM--

--THAT'S NOT--

YOU HAVE AGED YEARS IN THE WEEKS WE HAVE KNOWN EACH OTHER.

I JUST--

--I'M NOT AGING.

I KNOW WHAT HAS HAPPENED TO YOU.

THE STEPFORD SISTERS READ YOUR MIND...

...AND THEY TOLD ME.

WHY WOULD THEY DO THAT?

BECAUSE THEY WERE SCARED FOR YOU AND THOUGHT YOU NEEDED HELP...

...THIS WAS THEM TRYING TO HELP YOU.

SO IF YOU KNOW WHAT HAPPENED TO ME--

I WAS WAITING FOR YOU TO MUSTER UP THE COURAGE TO ASK FOR HELP.

YOU KNOW, PROFESSOR, EVER SINCE I MET YOU I'VE HEARD ALL THE STORIES, ABOUT HOW POLARIZING YOU ARE...

...HOW PEOPLE HATE YOU...

...AND I COULDN'T FOR THE LIFE OF ME FIGURE OUT WHAT THEY WERE TALKING ABOUT.

BECAUSE I THOUGHT YOU WERE PROBABLY THE MOST INTERESTING PERSON I'VE EVER MET!

UNTIL NOW.

NOW I SEE EXACTLY WHY YOU ANNOY PEOPLE.

EVA, SIT--

(OH YEAH, YELLING AFTER THEM NEVER WORKS.)

...YOU WERE ALSO RIGHT TO INVITE ME IN THE FIRST PLACE. I WANT IN.

IF NOT HERE, I'LL GO JOIN THAT OTHER SCHOOL THAT ISN'T HIDDEN IN THE CANADIAN WOODS OR WHEREVER THE HELL WE ARE.

STOP. YOU SAVED OUR LIVES WITHOUT EVEN THE SLIGHTEST HESITATION...

...YOU PUSHED YOURSELF AND YOUR POWERS AND YOU REVEALED A SOPHISTICATION THAT IS BOTH PROMISING AND A LITTLE SCARY.

YOU MEAN I'M MORE POWERFUL THAN BOTH OF US THOUGHT I WAS?

YEAH?

WELL, I'M MORE THAN A LITTLE SCARED.

PLEASE ACCEPT MY INVITATION TO REJOIN THIS GROUP.

HELL YEAH.

I NEED YOUR HELP.

AND WE NEED YOURS.

WELCOME BACK, X-MAN.

THAT'S A LOVELY MOMENT...

CELESTE, BE NICE.

NOW WHO'S GOING TO DEAL WITH THE POP STAR HAVING A MENTAL BREAKDOWN IN OUR BATHROOM?

DAZZLER, AGENT OF S.H.I.E.L.D.

NEWBERRY, SOUTH CAROLINA.
TODAY.

MATTHEW?

UM-- IT'S ME... ALANA.

I KNOW.

HOW ARE YOU? ARE YOU LIVING HERE NOW?

JEFF AND I--WE JUST MOVED HERE.

UM...

I WAS HOPING YOU'D KEEP IN TOUCH. I REALLY WAS.

YEAH-- I CALLED.

I KNOW, I JUST DIDN'T--

SHE WAS MY SISTER. THAT MAKES YOU MY BROTHER NO MATTER WHAT. YOU KNOW?

LISTEN, I JUST DON'T WANT TO TALK ABOUT THIS.

YOU JUST DISAPPEARED.

IT--IT--IT WAS GOOD SEEING YOU.

NO.

NO, MATTHEW, I JUST WANT TO TALK TO YOU.

L-LEAVE ME ALONE.

THIS ISN'T RIGHT. YOU NEED TO TALK TO ME.

I SAID NO!

SO WHAT'S IN THE WILL?

FIRST THINGS FIRST, BOBBY...

...I KNOW THIS IS A DELICATE QUESTION AND ONE I WOULD NOT NORMALLY HAVE TO ASK...

...BUT YOU ARE THE X-MEN AND YOU DON'T DO NORMAL.

IT APPEARS NOT.

TO THE BEST OF YOUR KNOWLEDGE...

...IS XAVIER REALLY DEAD?

I ONLY ASK BECAUSE WE BOTH KNOW THAT "DEAD" AND "DEAD" DEAD...

HE HAS--HE IS GONE.

IT'S A VALID QUESTION, THOUGH.

VALID QUESTION?

LEGALLY SPEAKING.

JUST READ THIS THING SO WE CAN GET ON WITH OUR LIVES.

I HATE THIS KIND OF STUFF. I JUST HATE IT.

IT STIPULATES THAT EVERYONE NAMED IN THE WILL BE PRESENT FOR THE READING OF THE WILL.

NO.

OF COURSE.

WHO?

SCOTT SUMMERS.

YOU GUYS KNOW WHERE HE IS?

BECAUSE YOU REALLY NEED HIM HERE.

RIGHT NOW.

24

JEAN GREY'S SCHOOL FOR GIFTED YOUNGSTERS.

BOBBY?

BOBBY? DID YOU HEAR ME?

ARE YOU ALL RIGHT?

YOU KNOW WHAT WE X-MEN ARE REALLY GOOD AT?

WE'RE REALLY GOOD AT KEEPING OURSELVES SUPER-BUSY SO WE DON'T HAVE TIME TO MOURN OUR LOSSES.

CHARLES XAVIER IS GONE.

CHARLES XAVIER.

AND WE SIT IN THE HOUSE HE BUILT FOR US AND WE JUST KEEP ON KEEPING ON... WE...

SO, UM, AS I WAS SAYING... SCOTT SUMMERS.

DO YOU GUYS HAPPEN TO KNOW WHERE HE IS?

I DO.

HENRY? YOU DO? SINCE WHEN?

OF COURSE I DO, ORORO.

I HAVE MUTANT-FINDING CEREBRO TECHNOLOGY THAT I HELPED INVENT.

I CALIBRATED IT TO LOOK FOR PEOPLE WHO WERE HIDING FROM IT.

HE CAN HIDE FROM THE WORLD BUT HE CAN'T HIDE FROM *ME*.

HE'S A FUGITIVE FROM JUSTICE AND AT LEAST PARTLY RESPONSIBLE FOR THE MURDER OF CHARLES XAVIER...

...YOU HATE HIM NOW. YOU HAVE MADE THAT ABUNDANTLY CLEAR.

AND NOW YOU TELL ME YOU KNOW WHERE HE IS AND YOU NEVER DID ANYTHING ABOUT IT OR TOLD US BECAUSE...

...BECAUSE I DON'T WANT TO LOOK AT HIM.

I DON'T WANT ANY MORE OF MY LIFE DICTATED BY THE ACTIONS OF THAT MAN.

I DON'T WANT MY LIFE TO BE HIS LIFE.

IS THAT SO HARD TO UNDERSTAND?

DO ANY OF YOU--

--DO YOU HAVE ANYONE IN YOUR LIFE LIKE THAT, MISS WALTERS?

DO YOU HAVE SOMEONE IN YOUR LIFE THAT YOU JUST *DO NOT WANT?*

I DON'T KNOW...

HEY, GUYS, WHAT'S GOING ON?

WHERE'D BOBBY GO?

AND WHAT IS THIS TALL, GREEN, LOVELY VISION DOING HERE?

OH KURT, YOU SAY THAT TO ALL THE HULKS.

WERE ANY OF YOU AWARE THAT HENRY KNOWS WHERE SCOTT SUMMERS' SECRET MUTANT TRAINING CAMP IS?

I WAS.

BUT I'M A PSYCHIC AND I'M NOSY.

OH. THAT'S-- YOU HAVE XAVIER'S WILL.

PLEASE DON'T READ MY MIND, MISS SUMMERS.

XAVIER'S WILL? WHAT DOES IT SAY?

I HAVEN'T READ IT YET.

BUT IT STIPULATES THAT THE FOLLOWING PEOPLE BE PRESENT...

WHAT COULD BE IN IT?

WOLVERINE OWNS THE SCHOOL PROPERTY.

ACTUALLY, THAT AIN'T TRUE.

LOGAN, WHERE HAVE YOU BEEN?

WHERE I GO.

WHAT DO YOU MEAN? YOU NO LONGER OWN THE PROPERTY TO THE SCHOOL?

A WHILE BACK, WHEN I WASN'T SO SURE THINGS WERE GOIN' MY WAY, I SIGNED IT ALL BACK OVER TO XAVIER.

JUST IN CASE.

AND IN THAT DOCUMENT-- THAT WILL TELL US WHO OWNS THE SCHOOL NOW?

GODDESS.

IT'S SCOTT.

SCOTT OWNS THE SCHOOL NOW.

WHAT?

XAVIER COULD NEVER IMAGINE THAT SCOTT SUMMERS, HIS FIRST AND BRIGHTEST STUDENT, A VIRTUAL SON, WOULD BE THE MAN WHO KILLED HIM.

SCOTT SUMMERS KILLED CHARLES XAVIER?

WELL, IT'S COMPLICATED.

NO.

IT'S NOT.

HE WASN'T IN CONTROL OF HIMSELF.

THE PHOENIX POSSESSED HIM.

I DID NOT KNOW THAT.

I STILL DO NOT BELIEVE IT.

AND NEITHER WOULD CHARLES.

HE LEFT THE SCHOOL TO HIM. I GUARANTEE IT.

WHAT DOES THAT MEAN FOR US?

IT MEANS WE'RE GONNA SETTLE THIS THING WITH SUMMERS ONCE AND FOR ALL.

WHAT-- WHAT IS THIS?

MY NAME IS MARIA HILL.

I'M THE COMMANDER OF S.H.I.E.L.D.

DO YOU KNOW WHAT THAT IS? DO YOU UNDERSTAND ME?

Y-YES. WHO AM I SPEAKING TO?

YOU'RE-- YOU'RE A ROBOT?

NO. I'M A HUMAN PERSON, BUT I'M SPEAKING TO YOU FROM A REMOTE LOCATION.

FOR SAFETY REASONS.

AND YOU ARE?

M-MATTHEW.

MATTHEW MALLOY.

MATTHEW...? DID YOU CREATE THIS SITUATION?

SITUATION?

DID YOU MAKE THIS MESS?

A POWER?

DO YOU HAVE-- ARE YOU A POWER?

YOU'RE NOT IN TROUBLE, I JUST WANT TO TALK--

DID I KILL THESE PEOPLE?!

THERE WERE PEOPLE.

HAVE YOU EVER DONE ANYTHING LIKE THIS BEFORE?

MATTHEW, IT WOULD BE WONDERFUL IF YOU WOULD CALMLY SIT DOWN.

ALL LIFE
SIGNS ARE
GONE.

WHAT
AM I?

SO, YOU... ...FOUND US.

SCOTT...

WHO IS IT?

IT'S ME, SCOTT. CALM DOWN.

ORORO?!

OH, MY GOD...

NICE PLACE YOU GOT HERE.

DID YOU IRONICALLY PUT YOURSELF IN JAIL?

OR SUB-CONSCIOUSLY?

SUBCONSCIOUSLY.

I SUPPOSE YOU'D LIKE TO KNOW WHAT WE ARE DOING HERE...

GET DRESSED, "SLIM." WE'LL BE WAITING OUTSIDE.

THE OLD MAN'S FINAL REQUEST.

WE WILL GLADLY GIVE YOU ALL A LIFT.

WE'LL FIND OUR OWN WAY.

I APPRECIATE YOU MAKING THE TRIP OUT HERE.

HOLD ON, ILLYANA...

NO. PLEASE RESPECT MY WISHES ON THIS. THE STUDENTS STAY.

YOU KNOW HE LEFT ME THE JEAN GREY SCHOOL, EMMA.

WHAT AM I SUPPOSED TO DO WITH IT?

THIS IS GOING TO BE *PROFOUNDLY* UNPLEASANT.

OR MAYBE THIS IS THAT ONE TIME IN THE HISTORY OF OUR HISTORY WHERE EVERYTHING IS JUST CHILL AND LOW KEY AND--

KITTY, PLEASE.

I KNOW. I COULDN'T EVEN FINISH THE SENTENCE.

ILLYANA...

...IF YOU WILL...

WHAT IF IT'S A TRAP AND THEY NEVER COME BACK?

WE'LL HAVE TO REPOPULATE THE MUTANT RACE THROUGH PROCREATION.

SO LET'S ALL GET TO WORK.

ALRIGHTY THEN.

YOU GUYS ARE SCARING ME.

25

"I KNOW SOME OF YOU HOLD ME IN A VERY HIGH REGARD AND FOR THAT I AM HUMBLED AND HONORED.

"AND IT IS BECAUSE OF THIS HIGH REGARD THAT I KNOW WHAT I AM ABOUT TO TELL YOU WILL SHOCK AND MAYBE *HORRIFY* SOME OF YOU.

"BUT PLEASE HEAR ME OUT UNTIL THE END.

"LET ME EXPLAIN MYSELF FULLY BEFORE YOU JUDGE TOO HARSHLY.

"THIS WAS MANY YEARS AGO...IT WAS IN THE XAVIER SCHOOL FOR GIFTED YOUNGSTERS' EARLIEST DAYS, AND I HAD FINALLY COME UP WITH A WORKING MODEL FOR CEREBRO...

"...COMBINING OUR MUTANT-SEEKING TECHNOLOGY WITH MY TELEPATHIC ABILITIES WAS FINALLY NOT JUST A THEORY BUT A REALITY.

"AT LONG LAST WE WOULD BE ABLE TO LOCATE ANY MUTANT IN NEED...

"...OR ANY MUTANT THAT WOULD BE A THREAT TO MAN OR TO OUR CAUSE OF HAVING MUTANTS AND HUMANS LIVING TOGETHER IN PEACE AND HARMONY.

"ONE DAY, WHILE THE ORIGINAL X-MEN WERE OUT ON A MISSION, I WAS USING CEREBRO TO ATTEMPT TO KEEP TABS ON MAGNETO AND OTHER SUCH CONCERNS, WHEN A VERY UNIQUE SIGNATURE APPEARED.

"SOMETHING I HAD NOT SEEN BEFORE.

"IT WAS MOST DEFINITELY A MUTANT SIGNATURE BUT THERE WAS SOMETHING...DIFFERENT, SOMETHING MORE POWERFUL...

"...AT FIRST I WAS WORRIED THAT THE MACHINE WAS BROKEN. THAT I HAD MISUSED IT.

"BUT IT WASN'T AND I HAD NOT.

"IT WAS THE LARGEST MUTANT POWER SIGNATURE CEREBRO HAD EVER REGISTERED.

"I WAS IMMEDIATELY FILLED WITH SUCH HOPE, SUCH A THRILL OF DISCOVERY...BUT THEN, SUDDENLY, A WAVE OF PANIC WASHED OVER ME.

"I COULDN'T BREATHE.

"WHAT IF MAGNETO FINDS THIS MUTANT BEFORE ME? WHAT IF HE IS ALREADY THERE?

"I COULDN'T GET A HOLD OF YOU X-MEN AND I COULDN'T WAIT FOR YOU TO RETURN FROM YOUR MISSION.

"I HAD TO SEE THIS MUTANT FOR MYSELF.

"I HAD TO GET THERE BEFORE ANYBODY ELSE."

"ONE WOULD THINK THAT I WOULD BE USED TO THE FACT THAT SO MANY EMERGING MUTANTS WERE SO YOUNG...

"...BUT THIS ONE WAS *SO* POWERFUL AND *SO* YOUNG.

"HE SEEMED SO...ORDINARY.

"HIS NAME WAS *MATTHEW MALLOY.*

"HE WAS EIGHT YEARS OLD."

MATTHEW
MALLOY.

TO BE
CONTINUED...

UNCANNY X-MEN #19 SKETCH VARIANT
BY J. SCOTT CAMPBELL

UNCANNY X-MEN #19 VARIANT
BY J. SCOTT CAMPBELL & NEI RUFFINO

ce to start reading the X-books."
— IGN.com

"This is the place to start reading the X-books" —IGN.com

ALL·NEW X·MEN

ALL-NEW X-MEN VOL. 1: YESTERDAY'S X-MEN PREMIERE HC
978-0-7851-6637-5 • OCT130757

"Beautiful and funny, heartfelt and intriguing."
— CBR.com

MARVEL
NOW!

© 2013 MARVEL